D0553306

The SS Great Britain Story

The SS Great Britain Story

John Christopher

The
History
Press

Published in the United Kingdom in 2011 by
The History Press
The Mill · Brimscombe Port · Stroud · Gloucestershire · GL5 2QG

British Library Cataloguing in Publication Data
A catalogue record for this book is available from the British
Library.

Hardback ISBN 978-0-7524-5604-1

➤ *The exterior has been
restored to its 1843
as-launched appearance.*

Typesetting and origination by The History Press
Printed in China

CONTENTS

ACKNOWLEDGEMENTS

Unless otherwise stated all new photography and some of the ship in the 1970s are by the author (JC). Other photographs of the salvage and restoration come from the archives of the former South West News Agency (SWNA) which are now owned by me. I must thank several other sources for providing images, including the SS *Great Britain* Trust (SSGB), the US Library of Congress (LoC) and Campbell McCutcheon (CMcC). Thanks also to my wife Ute for proofreading.

John Christopher

The SS *Great Britain* is one of the most important ships ever built, but it was not the first iron-hulled ship. Neither was it the first screw-driven ship, or even the first transatlantic steamship for that matter. No, the significance of the *Great Britain* – and let's drop the 'SS' prefix for the sake of clarity – is that it brought all of these elements together for the first time. The genius of Isambard Kingdom Brunel was to combine and adapt the best of the technology available, and the latest materials and manufacturing techniques, to create something that is much more than the sum of its parts. In this instance he created a blueprint that would influence

➤ *Each of Isambard Kingdom Brunel's three ships pushed forward the boundaries of ship-building.*

➤Built to Brunel's broad gauge, the Great Western Railway connected the cities of London and Bristol.

➤➤ This is how the Clifton Suspension Bridge might have looked if the money hadn't run out.

9

the design of all ocean liners to come, and in doing so he shaped our 'modern' concepts of international travel.

It was Brunel who foresaw a time when a traveller living in London could catch a train and go all the way to New York on one unified transportation system. It is said that this grand vision came to him during a meeting of the board of directors of the Great Western Railway. When one director complained about the inordinate length of the railway line, Brunel is said to have drawn upon his cigar and retorted, 'Why not make it longer, and have a steamboat go from Bristol to New York and call it the *Great Western*?' Said in jest or not, the result is that the Great Western Steamship Company was formed in 1836, with Brunel as engineer, of course. Bristol, the city which had given Brunel his most important engineering commissions

so far – the Clifton Suspension Bridge and the Great Western Railway – would be at the hub of this transport network. The new railway would deliver international travellers to Bristol, where they would stay overnight in the Great Western Hotel, before catching a steamship to New York the following morning.

▲ *The Great Western Hotel in Bristol, where travellers from London would stay overnight before departing by ship for New York.*

Did you know?

Brunel originally intended building the *Great Britain* as a wooden-hulled and paddle-powered ship similar to the *Great Western* of 1837.

At that time Bristol was a serious rival to Liverpool's bid to become the major transatlantic port, but a combination of factors, including the difficulties of navigating the River Avon's tidal excesses combined with the tardiness of the Bristol authorities in improving the dock facilities and their greed in charging exorbitant harbour fees, meant that neither of Brunel's Bristol-built steamships – the first being the *Great Western* and the second the *Great Britain* – would ever operate from their home port. The Great Western Hotel still stands in St George's Street, tucked behind the Bristol Council House, and the *Great Britain* itself has become the centrepiece of the revitalised city docks. One is a reminder of a lost transatlantic dream and the other a lasting tribute to Victorian engineering at its finest.

Only Brunel realised that it was possible to design a steamship which could carry enough coal for any given length of voyage. A transatlantic steamship was not an impossibility … but only a problem of correct proportion.

L.T.C. Rolt, *Isambard Kingdom Brunel*, 1957

Of all the high-profile engineers of the nineteenth century, Isambard Kingdom Brunel stood head and shoulders above his contemporaries. Putting aside the fact that he was only just over 5ft tall, and not forgetting his stove-pipe hat which, in truth, was no higher than was the fashion at the time, he was known as the 'Little Giant' because of his vision, tenacity and drive. None of the others, not the Stephensons or Telford, built railways, bridges *and* ocean liners. Born in 1806, a little over thirty years before Victoria became queen, Brunel had the good fortune to be on the scene at the moment when iron and steam came together to create an era of unprecedented change in transportation. It was nothing short of a technological revolution, one that cut great swathes across the landscape

▼ *The emblems on the ship's prow represent the arts and industries of her birthplace and intended home port, Bristol.*

Suspension Bridge – unfinished because the money had run out – and built the Great Western Railway, arguably the finest in the world. So it was little wonder that he should then apply his 'can-do' attitude to the design and construction a trio of 'great' ships, the *Great Western*, *Great Britain* and the *Great Eastern*.

The first of these, the *Great Western*, was envisaged as a means of extending the railway line from London to Bristol via transatlantic steamship all the way to New York. In January 1836 the Great Western Steamship Company (GWSC) was formed with Brunel as its unpaid engineer. However, it is fair to say that with the first ship, the *Great Western*, his role was more supervisory than hands-on designer. It was the Bristol shipbuilder William Patterson who provided the expertise and experience

and reshaped our towns and cities. By the late 1830s the young Brunel was riding this wave of success. At the top of his powers he had already designed the Clifton

needed to build such a large wooden-hulled ship, and at 212ft long and with a displacement of 2,300 tons it was to be bigger than any other ship afloat. This was pushing oak construction to its limits and great emphasis was placed on longitudinal

➤ The iron structure of the hull laid bare in the early stages of the Great Britain's *restoration in the mid-1970s. (JC)*

strengthening provided by iron diagonals and a row of iron bolts running the full length. This was to prevent hogging, the tendency of a longer ship to sag if not fully supported by the water in rougher seas. The paddle-driven *Great Western* was launched in Bristol, from a slipway near the Prince Street Bridge, on 19 July 1837. Although the *Great Western* wasn't the first steamship to cross the Atlantic, it did put to rest widely held concerns that a steamship couldn't carry enough coal for the long trip. In the event, the ship proved successful enough for the GWSC to commission a second vessel.

Originally Brunel had envisioned another paddle-driven wooden ship – a bigger version of the *Great Western*. The African oak was purchased and the ship had a name, the *City of New York*. Iron would

be cheaper and stronger than wood, it would even be lighter because an iron hull is thinner, but Brunel's main concern was that the iron might throw out the ship's compass. Then, in 1838, the iron-hulled *Rainbow* arrived in Bristol, equipped with a system of correcting magnets to rectify this problem and Brunel readily swapped to iron for his new ship. And when the *Archimedes* came to town the following year, pushed by an experimental screw propeller devised by Francis Pettit Smith, he scrapped the half-built paddles. Throughout his career Brunel was never afraid to adopt other people's good ideas when it suited, and the *Great Britain* – as the ship eventually became known – represents a highly successful amalgamation of engineering innovations.

The hull is clinker-built, constructed of iron plates forged at the Ironbridge foundry

◀ *The hull is clinker built with wrought iron plates cast in a foundry and then shaped on site.*

Did you know?
The first working name for the ship was *City of New York*, although this later became the *Mammoth* and it was finally christened as the *Great Britain*. It was the second of Brunel's three 'Great' ships.

A throwback to earlier ships, the hull featured 'faux' gunwales. These were painted out after the first refit.

One of the first sights to welcome visitors to the ship is the transom, with its decorative carvings featuring the coat of arms for Bristol.

at Coalbrookdale in Shropshire and then shipped down the Severn to Bristol. Each plate was about 6ft by 2ft 6in and was individually shaped and riveted in position, overlapping horizontally and connected on the inside by iron straps. Constructing the ship of iron required a rethink of traditional timber shipbuilding methods. For a start, a 322ft-long ship needed great rigidity to overcome the hogging problem and accordingly the hull was fitted with ten iron girders running its full length, a double bottom, five bulkheads to create watertight compartments and two longitudinal bulkheads up to main deck level. Diagonal iron deck beams and iron stringer plates gave it the strength of a box girder. The result was a massively strong hull, and a very graceful one too seen from underneath. The extent to which the hull bulges outwards was dictated by the wider engines needed to drive the screw propeller – see *Engines and Propeller Power*.

This bulge also creates more internal space, while the bows of the ship are as sharp as any fast clipper. When completed, the ship was 50ft 6in wide and had a displacement of 3,400 tons, exceeding that of any other vessel at that time by 1,000 tons. Along with 120 passengers and a crew of 120, she could carry 1,200 tons of cargo and 1,200 tons of coal. It should be remembered that the *Great Britain* was designed as a sail-assisted steamship and accordingly it was fitted with six schooner-style iron masts to take advantage of favourable winds. It was the first ship to be registered as such, although, strictly speaking, the rig consisted of one square-sailed mast and five schooner. This

configuration defied existing terminology and the masts were named after the days of the week, starting from the front.

GENERAL ARRANGEMENT OF THE SHIP

It would be an endless task and without the aid of drawings a fruitless one to attempt a description of this magnificent vessel. I can however state that her lines are very beautiful and adapted to the highest rates of speed. The general character of the workmanship is very good and does a great credit to the builder.

John Grantham, during construction, 1842

The engine bay neatly divides the ship internally into two main spaces. The rear or after accommodation was for the first-class passengers, with the promenade on the upper between deck, cabins to either side, plus dining saloon and more cabins on the lower deck. The space forward of the engine was used in a similar fashion for the second-class passengers and the forecastle, or fo'c'sle, provided accommodation for the crew. The lowest level, the hold, was used for storing the coal and cargo. Following its return to Bristol in 1970, the *Great Britain* has been restored to reflect various periods during its time in service, but in the main it follows the original 1843 layout and this description conforms with this.

For the Victorian passenger, or for the modern visitor for that matter, the ship is entered via the weather deck. Unlike modern practices on ocean liners this is remarkably flat and open with no significant structures to speak of, although it is cluttered with numerous skylights, the windlass mechanism and the hut-like entrances to the lower decks. The weather deck was very much a working area for the ship's crew, and the open railings served to allow sea water to run off the deck. It was also an outdoor space for the passengers. Just aft of the funnel and the engine compartment is a white line running between either side of the deck. A sign warns, 'First class passengers only beyond this point'. Whatever their class, passengers venturing on to the weather deck were exposed to the elements, especially with the ship at full pelt, whether this was the wind and the rain or the heat of the sun, although it was possible to rig up simple canvas awnings.

While on the weather deck, note the shed housing a cow. Several animals were carried on a long voyage, including cows for their milk and other animals for meat. Horses were not normally carried, except when the *Great Britain* was used as a troopship to the Crimea and India. Towards the stern and behind a large circular skylight the ship's wheel is positioned just behind a binnacle holding the ship's compass. There is no permanent protection for the steersman, and likewise the bridge is exactly what its name suggests, a simple open bridge or

The huge windlass mechanism on the forward part of the weather deck.

walkway running from side to side behind the funnel to provide all-round visibility of the ship. Rising above the deck are the six tall masts which are flying the same pennants today as when the ship was launched. The masts are not vertical, but lean backwards slightly which gives the ship an incidental 'go-faster' stance.

Heading down the steps to the upper 'tween decks it takes a moment for your eyes to become accustomed to the comparative darkness. That changes on the

➤ *Leading off from the promenade, the ladies' boudoir where the women could relax in a degree of privacy.*

first-class promenade saloon in the rear half of the ship. This impressive room, 110ft long and 22ft across at its widest point, is brightly illuminated thanks to the rows of skylights. These are mimicked by matching light wells arranged along the floor on either side to take some daylight down to the deck below. Towards the stern there is the large circular skylight and at the back of the saloon the passengers were able to observe the tiller mechanism (now covered over). The sense of airiness is enhanced by the décor, as described by *The Evening Post* in 1845:

The walls of the after or principle promenade saloon are painted in delicate tints and along the sides are carved chairs of oak. A row of well proportioned pillars which range down the side of the promenade serve the double purpose of ornament to the room and support the deck. In this saloon, either side, is a range of exceedingly comfortable state rooms and sleeping berths.

◄ *A typical two-berth cabin.*

Did you know?
The Great Western Dry Dock which houses the *Great Britain* was specifically excavated for the ship's construction in 1839. It gets its name from the Great Western Steamship Company.

The cabins leading off from the promenade were arranged two deep to provide forty-four berths. They might look cramped to us, but these were the best and certainly the most spacious cabins on the entire ship. Each was equipped with bunk beds and a washstand, and those on the outer side benefited from a small porthole. At the forward end of these cabins there was a ladies' boudoir fitted with a long settee, where the women could relax with a degree of privacy. The captain's sleeping berth and some of the stewardesses' cabins were also situated off the promenade.

Immediately beneath the promenade saloon was the dining saloon on the lower 'tween deck, an equally sumptuously appointed public area, although somewhat darker, lacking the direct daylight. Artificial lighting was most probably provided by

◄ The sumptuously decorated first-class dining saloon on the lower 'tween deck.

▲ Meal times were an important part of the daily routine on a long voyage. This is the ship's well-equipped galley or kitchen.

This is really a beautiful room … Its fittings are alike chaste and elegant. Down the centre are principal columns of white and gold with ornamental capitals of great beauty. Some looking glasses are so arranged as to reflect the saloon lengthwise, at two opposite sides, from which a very pleasing illusion is produced.

Interestingly, there is no indication of how the public spaces might have been heated and there are comments by passengers which suggest that it could be quite cold at times. On the other hand, the heat of the tropical sun on the iron hull could make the interior uncomfortably hot. In its day the accommodation was regarded very favourably, as observed by the *New York Daily Tribune*: 'We admired the plain and solid style adopted in all parts of the *Great*

△ *The cramped accommodation for steerage passengers has been recreated in the forward part of the ship.*

napthene lamps. The saloon was arranged with three dining tables running lengthwise, with space for 228 diners at a time, and the benches had backs which could be flipped to face the table or into the open spaces in between. As one contemporary description stated:

Britain, so simple, so judicious, so easily kept clean, so truly English!'

The space forward of the engine bay was arranged in a similar but less extravagant manner for the other passengers, although this has not been recreated in the modern restoration.

ENGINES AND PROPELLER POWER

> If there is anything objectionable in the construction or machinery of this noble ship, it is the mode of propelling her by screw propeller; and we should not be surprised if it should be, ere long, superseded by paddle wheels.
>
> *Scientific America*, on the ship's arrival in New York in 1845

Although Brunel was not the creator of the screw-propulsion concept, he did more than anyone to ensure its successful application, particularly through his development work for the *Great Britain*. As mentioned, the original plan was to build the ship as a larger version of the *Great Western* – in wood and with paddle-wheels. However, by the time the dry dock was ready and construction could begin on the new ship, the choice of construction materials had been changed from wood to wrought iron.

Regardless of this change, it was still to be a paddle-steamer at this point, albeit the biggest the world had ever seen, and tenders were invited for the construction of the ship's great engines. The engineering company Maudsley, Sons & Field, who had built the engines for the *Great Western*, were Brunel's preferred choice but the GWSC favoured a lower tender from a young engineer named Francis Humphrys. It soon became obvious that the sheer scale of the project created a whole new set of problems that would require new solutions. For starters, there wasn't a hammer in the world that was big enough to forge the main drive shaft for the paddles. Humphrys called upon his friend James Nasmyth for

> ➤ *This large skylight above the engine bay gave passengers a reassuring view of the mighty steam engine at work.*

Replica of the original six-bladed propeller, photographed in the mid-1970s when the wooden rudder was still in place. (JC)

help and as a result Nasmyth invented his steam hammer. It was a typical example of one of Brunel's ambitious projects sending out a ripple of progress that would spread throughout the engineering and industrial world.

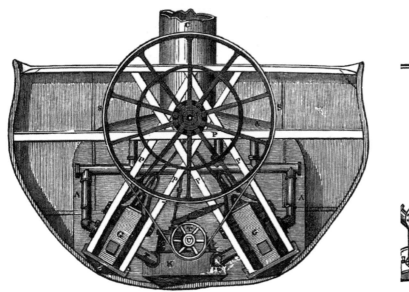

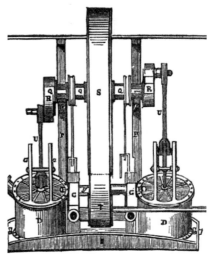

For poor Humphrys the project took another sharp turn. In May 1840 the experimental screw-driven *Archimedes* arrived in Bristol. This small vessel was being taken on a promotional tour by its creator, Francis Pettit Smith, and Brunel was an immediate convert. He was well aware that paddle-wheels are inefficient in

⌃ *This detailed scale model of the steam engine is on display in the museum.*

rougher seas as they lift in and out of the water with every roll of the hull. This also put a stress on the engines each time the paddle-boards hit the water. By December 1840, Brunel recommended that the new ship should be solely propeller driven. Alas, this blow seems to have been too much for the disappointed Humphrys, who is said to have died from the strain. Meanwhile, the company directors agreed to give Brunel and Pettit Smith the time they needed to perfect the screw-propulsion system and work halted on the ship for over two years while further tests were conducted.

The Royal Navy was also becoming interested in the screw and they commissioned the two engineers to develop designs and undertake trials for a new naval vessel. The *Rattler*, an 800-ton sloop with engines supplied by Maudsleys, was launched in April 1843 and began a series of tests to determine the best form of propeller. Following on from the *Archimedes*, the first designs were longer screws, almost 6ft long and only 1ft 3in wide, but through experimentation this gradually changed to a flatter design with a greater diameter. Little by little, and at the expense of the Admiralty, the shape and number of blades were refined to the point where a shortened three-blade screw could achieve over 9 knots, which was far in excess of the Admiralty's expectations. For the far bigger *Great Britain* Brunel devised two alternative screws, a six-bladed screw made up of welded iron blades and a four-bladed one of cast bronze. The six-blade screw was fitted initially, but this

A view of the engine compartment from the upper 'tween deck looking back towards the huge chain wheel.

The replica steam engine has been constructed using modern lightweight materials to minimise loading on the ship's hull.

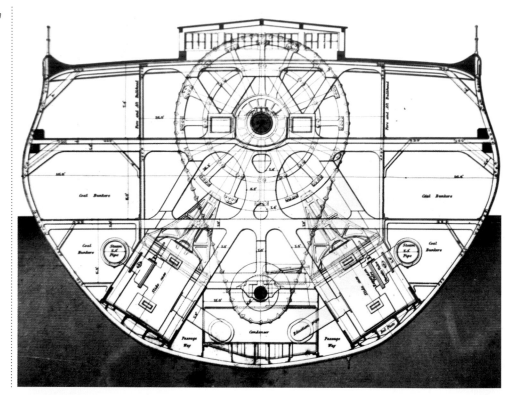

➤➤ *The spinning chain wheel on the replica engine.*

➤ *This contemporary diagram of the steam engine clearly shows the inverted 'V' of the cylinders.*

broke up on the second voyage and the cast screw was fitted in its place. Further significant changes to the propeller and rudder followed during the *Great Britain*'s later career – see *Australia Bound*.

The change from paddles to screw meant changes to the ship's steam engines and the transmission of power. With Humphrys out of the picture, Brunel oversaw the design of new engines in collaboration with Thomas Guppy, who was also in charge of their construction. The old paddle-driven steamships had relied upon low-speed machinery, but the screw needed to turn much faster. Instead of conventional beam engines, Brunel drew upon his father's work on a V-formation in which the cylinders drove upwards to a crankshaft. Today, visitors to the ship can see a very realistic reconstruction of the original 1,000hp

Beneath a sea of glass, a new sub-aquatic world has been created beneath the ship.

Did you know?

An iron hull is lighter than a wooden one because the iron plate is much thinner, and by the time of the SS *Great Britain*'s construction iron was becoming cheaper than timber.

engines. Unlike on a modern ship, where the engines are hidden out of view deep within the hull, the *Great Britain*'s engines – the beating, living heart of the steamship – are in full sight. This was done deliberately to reassure the passengers, who could marvel at their working. Weighing in at 340 tons, they occupy the full height of the three decks, with daylight provided by a large viewing canopy on the weather deck. Four 88in-diameter cylinders, sitting low in the hull at 33 degrees to the vertical, drive the large crankshaft set high in the engine compartment. The crankshaft turns at 18rpm, but via the chain drive this is converted to 53rpm on the propeller shaft to propel the ship at 12 knots or around 14mph (22km/h).

The *Great Britain*'s 1843 engines were taken out and replaced by smaller and more efficient ones in 1852. These, in turn, were removed when she was converted to a sailing ship in the 1880s – see *Windjammer*.

As a historical footnote, Brunel's third and final ship, the *Great Eastern*, was configured with both screws and paddles. This was because screws on their own would have been too big and the paddles were needed to manoeuvre this vast 692ft vessel in shallower harbour waters.

◄ *Twice the size of the Great Britain, Brunel's third and final ship, the Great Eastern, featured propellers and paddle-wheels. The latter were needed for manoeuvrability in shallower harbour waters.*

The vessel was decorated with the colours of all nations and as far as the eye could reach in every direction nothing was to be seen but flags, banners and emblems, and congregated masses of human beings … From the water's edge upwards rose tier above tier of spectators … Brandon Hill covered with not less than 30,000 spectators.

Illustrated London News, report of the launch, July 1843

The date of 19 July 1843 was selected to launch the *Great Britain* as it was the sixth anniversary of the launch of its predecessor, the *Great Western* steamship. Prince Albert travelled down from London by royal train, broad gauge of course. Along with 520 invited guests – including Brunel's father Marc – plus thousands of onlookers, he watched as Mrs Miles, the wife of one of the GWSC directors who had also launched the *Great Western*, stepped forward to name the ship. Originally referred to as the *City of New York*, the huge 322ft-long iron monster had become known as the *Mammoth* during her construction and only towards completion was this changed to the *Great Britain*.

Unfortunately, by the time Mrs Miles swung the champagne bottle at the ship's bow the steam packet *Avon* had started to tow the ship out into the floating harbour and the bottle fell short of its target. The prince intervened and hastily obtained another bottle which he hurled at the hull, showering the hapless workmen below with bubbly and glass. The crowds roared their approval and amid a cacophony of cheering, cannon fire, musical bands and

> *Resplendent in the Great Western Dry Dock, the* Great Britain *has become the centrepiece of the city dock's revival.*

church bells, the *Great Britain* was eased out of her dock.

The spectacle was unprecedented. Here was the grandest and largest vessel ever

seen, built and launched in Bristol by the most brilliant engineer of the age. The queen had only been on the throne for seven years and for the new Victorians this must have been the equivalent of the moon landings and the maiden flight of Concorde all rolled into one. If only the *Great Britain*'s departure from Bristol could have been a little less farcical.

The trouble was that Brunel's iron ship was too big for her home port. It is a bit like those stories of enthusiasts who build an aeroplane in their garage and then realise that the doors are too small to get it out. They usually end up demolishing the garage and that, more or less, is what happened with the *Great Britain*. When work first started on the ship, the Bristol Dock Company had promised to improve the entrances to the Cumberland Basin,

which acted as a large lock leading out to the tidal River Avon. If Bristol was ever to compete with Liverpool as a major port for larger ships it was vital that this work was carried out. But, in the event, the authorities had dragged their heels and now the *Great Britain* risked becoming stuck in the harbour. The ship's great length was not a problem provided she could be moved out through the locks and on to the river in one movement, but her width was. The final hull shape was wider than originally planned to accommodate the screw propeller and the engines had been installed in situ in the dry dock, which caused the ship to ride slightly lower than initially planned.

It was decided to make an attempt to move her out to the river on the high tide on the morning of 11 December 1844, with agreement from the Dock Company to temporarily remove some of the masonry

◀ *Close-up of the ship's decorative prow. Note the gunwale for the anchor chain.*

from the side walls of the locks to allow her through. Even so, she quickly became jammed in the lower lock and had to be swiftly hauled back into the basin to allow the lock gates to be shut. Failure to have done this would have left her stranded high and dry as the basin emptied with the ebbing tide – the damage could have

been considerable. That evening the tides were slightly higher and after more of the coping stones had been torn away from the lock walls, the *Great Britain* left Bristol for the first and final time. Clearly if it had been this difficult to get her out of Bristol's floating harbour there was absolutely no prospect of her returning to the city on a

Did you know?

On her maiden voyage to New York, in July 1845, the *Great Britain* sailed with only forty-five passengers on board as the public remained sceptical about the safety of an ocean-going vessel built of iron.

regular basis, and suggestions that docking facilities could be provided at Avonmouth fell on deaf ears.

As the *Great Britain* headed through the Avon Gorge down towards the Severn Estuary, her boilers were fired up and the six-bladed screw bit into the waters for the first time. The official sea trials commenced in January 1845, and on 20 January she made a round trip under steam to Ilfracombe at a very satisfactory average speed of over 11 knots. A few days later she was taken up the Thames and docked at Blackwall for several months while the final fitting out was completed. Just as in Bristol, the largest ship ever built attracted considerable attention from Londoners, including Queen Victoria who was given a guided tour. On leaving she commented to the captain, 'I am very much gratified by the sight of your magnificent ship and I wish you every possible success on your voyages across the Atlantic.'

The *Great Britain* finally reached Liverpool on 3 July 1845, almost two years after her launch, and preparations began in earnest for the first screw-driven crossing to New York and with it the dawn of a new age in transatlantic liners.

The kitchen is most completely fitted out with every conceivable apparatus for roasting boiling frying grilling and stewing, showering forth to all who can on a sea voyage enjoy them, a series of excellent and tempting dinners.

Chambers Edinburgh Journal, 1845

The first transatlantic voyage of the *Great Britain* began from Liverpool on 26 July 1845. Several years late into service, due mainly to the fundamental changes in her design and construction, she was by no means the first steamship service to New York. After all, the *Great Western* had already established the viability of this route and the *Great Britain* only had to follow its predecessor's success. Yet despite enormous interest in the new ship, on that first voyage she sailed with under fifty passengers on board and only 360 tons of cargo. It would take time before public concerns about the screw-driven ship of iron were dispelled.

There was bad weather in the mid-Atlantic, followed by thick fog near the American coast, but after fourteen days and twenty-one hours the *Great Britain* arrived at New York to a tumultuous reception from the excited crowds who had been eagerly awaiting her. Captain James Hosken told the American newspaper reporters that the voyage had been uneventful and that the passengers all seemed pleased with the accommodation and the lack of vibration in comparison with a paddle ship. In truth this wasn't the case as the ship had a tendency to roll, except when held stiff by the sails. Over the next nineteen days,

➤ *The* Great Britain
as transatlantic liner
complete with six masts.
These were named after
the days of the week.
(LoC)

while she was provisioned for the return trip, around 21,000 New Yorkers took the opportunity to look it over the ship for the privilege of parting with 25 cents a head. One American publication described her as 'truly beautiful', and another as 'the greatest maritime curiosity ever seen in the harbour'. However, other journalists were less enthusiastic: 'The bed linen looked uninviting, and the whole appearance of the cabins, whatever may have been their original splendour, was to us, greasy and smirchy.'

On 30 August, the *Great Britain* started out on the homeward leg of her voyage, with fifty-three passengers this time, plus a

One of the larger family cabins off the first-class promenade saloon.

cargo including 1,200 bales of cotton. For Captain Hosken there was an unexpected problem when it became clear that a number of crewmen had deserted to stay in New York. Consequently, he was short-handed on the return trip and as a result the topmast was snapped because there were insufficient men to take in the topsail in squally conditions. Two seamen were seriously injured in the incident and one had to have his arm amputated by the ship's surgeon; an unimaginably unpleasant procedure with the very limited medical resources available at sea. In sympathy the passengers had a whip-round and presented him with £25.

On the technical side, the boilers gave some trouble when they failed to supply adequate steam pressure and it was only thanks to the favourable winds that the ship

was safely back in Liverpool after a fifteen-day crossing. So far, so good. The *Nautical Magazine* had nothing but praise for the ship's revolutionary propulsion system: 'The vibration so generally complained of in paddle-steamers is scarcely felt in the *Great Britain*, even in the sternmost of the vessel.' But there were still nagging concerns about whether the iron hull might throw out the compass.

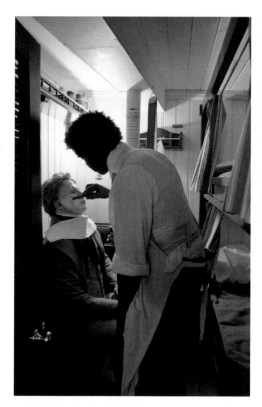

SECOND VOYAGE TO AMERICA

On the second trip westwards the passenger numbers had almost doubled to 102, although this was still far short of the 360 she was designed to carry. From the start they ran into some appalling weather and the foremast was carried clean away. Furthermore, Captain Hosken had managed to scrape the bottom on the Nantucket shoals, severely damaging the propeller. In a dry dock in New York the underside was

Did you know?

Although primarily powered by its steam engines, the *Great Britain* was provided with secondary sail power as was the custom with steamships at that time.

 In one of the first-class cabins a gentleman is shaved by his servant.

inspected. It was found that two propeller blades had been lost and the engineers removed another to restore the propeller's balance. Unfortunately, on the return voyage a propeller blade began striking the rudder gear. The engines were put in reverse and after 'two or three good thumps' the offending blade broke off. The other blades followed and the *Great Britain* limped home without steam and on wind power alone.

Over the winter a fairly major refit was carried out to fix the propeller and remedy some of the other teething problems. The spare four-bladed cast propeller was installed, improvements were made to the air pumps to increase the efficiency of the boilers and two additional bilge keels were fitted to reduce the rolling. Above decks,

◀ Injuries were commonplace among a ship's crew and here the surgeon deals with an injured hand.

The cabins were compact and the bunks were very narrow, but when not sleeping the passengers would spend most of their time in the public areas.

one mast behind the funnel was removed as the sails tended to burn and the iron rigging lines gave way to more traditional hemp rope.

Cosmetically the ship also had a facelift as the antiquated white bands running its length were painted out to create a smarter all-black upper hull.

THIRD TRANSATLANTIC ROUND-TRIP

When the ship sailed again, in May 1846, there were only twenty-eight bookings. Four days out from Liverpool an air pump fractured and the engine had to be shut down for six days while repairs were carried out. Once the pump had been fixed it was a trouble-free crossing. The return trip was the fastest yet at thirteen days and at one stage the ship achieved an average speed over a twenty-four-hour period of 13 knots. This was celebrated by the *Bristol Mirror* as 'a speed never before attained and never equalled on the ocean by any paddle-steamer or by any sailing vessel whatever'.

For the passengers who sailed on those first three voyages it must have been a curious experience, rattling about on the largest and most advanced ocean liner

The ship's bursar was responsible for carefully governing the distribution of the supplies.

An iron bath on an iron ship.

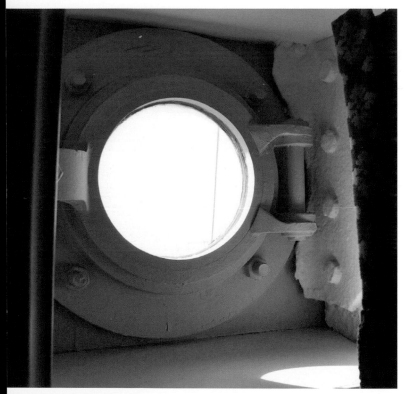

in the world and, in most cases, outnumbered by the crew. Consequently, there was little chance of getting a true flavour of the transatlantic experience, but on the whole everyone had been pleased with the ship's performance. Clearly it was time for the *Great Britain* to settle down into a routine of reliable service if she was ever going to pay her way. The construction and subsequent refit had both been enormously expensive, and bad news came for the GWSC directors when they learned that they had lost out to Cunard on lucrative transatlantic mail contracts. They urgently needed some good luck.

◀ *One of the* Great Britain's *portholes.*

I was grieved to see this fine ship lying unprotected, deserted and abandoned by all those who ought to know her value, and ought to have protected her … the finest steamship in the world, in excellent condition, such that £4,000 or £5,000 would repair all the damage done, has been left, and is lying, like a useless saucepan on the most exposed shore you can imagine.

I.K. Brunel, on seeing the ship aground at Dundrum Bay, 1846

On 22 September 1846 the *Great Britain* departed from Liverpool on her second voyage of the second transatlantic season. In command was Captain Hosken and, as before, his first task was to take the ship across the Irish Sea, around the southern tip of the Isle of Man, and to navigate northwards through the gap between the Irish mainland and the Isle and then via the North Channel out into the Atlantic. There were 180 passengers on board this time – still only half capacity – and most were settling down for their first night at sea when disaster struck. At a little after 9.30p.m. there was a terrible shuddering and lurching as the hull scraped across gravel. They had run aground at Dundrum Bay in County Down. It is said that Hosken had been misled by an error on the new charts causing confusion in the identification of a new light on the island, but it may be that the iron hull had affected the ship's compass. Either way, the captain had lost his bearings and it was only with the coming of dawn that he realised where they had ended up. Miraculously, at least they had missed the rocks.

During that fearful night the sea repeatedly broke over the ship with a noise

Did you know?
The newly built ship was notorious for its tendency to roll, especially without the calming influence of the sails in calmer weather, and bilge keels were added on either side of the hull to reduce this.

A view of the cluttered weather deck looking towards the stern. The open platform of the bridge is just behind the funnel.

Reconstruction of a well-appointed cabin in the forward half of the ship.

like thunder. One lady passenger later gave a dramatic account of the scene: 'There was the throwing overboard of the coals, the cries of children, the groans of women, the blue lights, the signal guns, even the tears of men and amidst all rose the voice of prayers.' In the morning, a procession of carts came out over the sands to the stricken ship and the passengers and their belongings were taken to safety. For the *Great Britain* there was no easy fix and initial attempts to lighten the ship in order

to float her off failed. By the end of the month Brunel's trusted colleague, Captain Christopher Claxton, arrived on the scene and, having failed in one further attempt to refloat the ship, he set the sails to drive the hull further up the beach in order to save her from the worst of the waves. They would have to sit it out over the winter to wait for the higher spring tides. Attempts to create protective breakwaters were fruitless, and by the time a very busy Brunel was able to get over to Ireland in early December he was aghast at what he saw.

He immediately set to work on a solution. To ensure that the currents did not wash the sand away, thus threatening to break her back, large faggots or bundles of beech saplings, lashed together with iron rods and further weighted down with iron weights, were arranged to protect the exposed stern and to create a breakwater. It was difficult work and the faggots were frequently washed away at first, but Brunel was in fighting mood and urged his team to double their efforts. By early spring the ship was further lightened to raise the bow on wedges to allow repairs to be made to the dented and leaking bottom. And then they had to wait for the highest tides to lift her

◄ One of the more spacious cabins.

◀ Brunel was appalled that the ship had been left almost unprotected and he devised a flexible breakwater to protect it from the waves.

▼ The scene at Dundrum Bay prior to the ship being floated off. Note the four-bladed propeller.

sufficiently to clear the reefs which blocked the way back to the deep waters. Finally, in late August 1847 and after eleven long months of being stranded, the tides rose by more than 15ft and the *Great Britain* was floated off the beach and taken in tow back to Liverpool for repairs.

It is unlikely that any other ship could have survived this prolonged ordeal – a vindication of Brunel's construction methods – but its salvation had come at a price. The *Great Britain* was saved, but the Great Western Steamship Company was financially ruined in the process. Brunel's vision of a unified transatlantic service by which passengers would be conveyed by train and ship all the way from London to New York was in tatters. The company directors had already sold the *Great Western* steamship in April 1847 and they were left with no other option but to sell the *Great Britain* too. She was put up for auction in Liverpool in September 1848 but failed to attract bids up to the reserve price of £4,000. Eventually she was sold in December 1850 to Gibbs, Bright & Co. for the sum of £18,000 – a fraction of the £120,000 which she had cost to build three years earlier. At least she had avoided the fate of becoming a wreck at Dundrum, and Brunel's iron ship would soon enjoy a new lease of life under her new owners. Gold had been discovered on the other side of the world and the *Great Britain* was Australia bound.

➤ Illustrated London News *engraving of the salvage operation at Dundrum.*

That any person being drunk and disorderly shall have his name given to the barman, who is to supply him with nothing more for the remainder of the voyage. All singing, card playing and other amusements calculated to disturb the peace of the night to cease by 10.00pm.

Ship's Rules and Regulations, on the Australian service, 1854

Following on from the sale of the ship to Gibbs, Bright & Co., the *Great Britain* underwent her most extensive refit, this time to adapt her for the lucrative Australian run. Gold had been found in Victoria and there was a rush of emigrants keen to grab their share, but there were not enough suitable vessels available to meet the sudden increase in demand. It wasn't just a matter of increasing the capacity to carry more passengers and cargo, but also to extend the range of the ship as the 12,000-mile run to Melbourne was beyond a sail-assisted steamship without the expense of re-coaling en route.

In addition to repairs and strengthening of the hull, the principal modifications saw the original engines removed and replaced by smaller and more efficient oscillating engines built by John Penn & Sons of Greenwich. There had been considerable progress in engine development in the few years since the *Great Britain* had been built. Along with the old engines, out went the cumbersome chain-gear drive, the three boilers and the single funnel. In their place were fitted a cog-wheel arrangement to drive the propeller shaft, six smaller boilers operating at twice the pressure and a pair of funnels situated side by side. The four-

> *Following an all-too-brief stint as a transatlantic liner, the* Great Britain *enjoyed a more successful second career on the Australia run.*

After the second refit the ship had additional accommodation on the top deck, new engines, twin funnels and only four masts. (LoC)

Did you know?

The hull of the ship has been restored to its launch colours in black with false gunwales or gun holes painted in white – a throwback to earlier naval colour schemes.

bladed propeller was changed for a cast three-blade model, and the existing sail plan was altered to four masts, providing increased sail area with two of the masts square-rigged. Passenger capacity was upped from 360 to 730, most notably

by adding an additional 300ft-long deck house built on top of the existing weather deck and by creating more cabins on the 'tween decks, including increased 'steerage' accommodation. They were creating the Victorian equivalent of the modern no-frills budget airline.

The ship returned to service in May 1852, initially on a shake-down transatlantic voyage, and three months later she made the first trip to Australia. In charge of the Australia runs was Captain Mathews, not a popular man among the passengers or crew by all accounts. The first trip to Melbourne took eighty-three days, instead of the anticipated sixty, after strong headwinds had forced Mathews to turn back to St Helena at one stage in order to take on more coal. On the return trip it became clear that the modifications had not gone far enough for

the longer runs to Australia. The *Great Britain* could not rely on steam power augmented by sail and instead it had to become a steam-assisted sailing ship. Accordingly, the rig was altered to three conventional sailing masts. In addition, a novel system for raising the propeller to reduce resistance in the water when under sail, which had been added on the first refit, was modified with a two-bladed lifting screw.

A contemporary engraving of a crowded emigrant ship bound for Australia. (LoC)

A four-berth cabin.

➤ *Typically crowded accommodation in steerage. Note the sleeping cat under the bunk.*

➤➤ *The most southern part of the route to Australia often took the ship among the icebergs.*

Over the next twenty-four years the ship settled into its new role and made a total of twenty-two return trips to Australia. Making full use of the trade winds, the journey generally took around sixty days, heading down through the eastern Atlantic, around the Cape of Good Hope and across the southern Indian Ocean to Australia, and back across the South Pacific and around Cape Horn and back across the Atlantic. With favourable winds this journey could be accomplished in as little as fifty-five days.

If you visit the *Great Britain* today you will find that the upper accommodation deck added for the Australian run has gone, and the masts and rudder are also as originally designed, as is the replica of the first engine. But if you head forward from the engine bay one area of steerage accommodation gives some idea of the

sort of conditions many of the emigrants to Australia would have experienced on board. Just forward of the ship's galley is an area of small, very basic cabins just big enough for two bunk beds, a small shelf and somewhere to hang a lamp. Beyond these is the most basic accommodation, with dark, narrow corridors of bunk beds. Life for these passengers would have been cramped and uncomfortable. There was no privacy to talk off and a host of rules prohibited anti-social behaviour, including drunkenness or fighting. However, in general, there was a great sense of community on board.

Just as back in England, life on board ship was very different for the upper classes of passengers, to the extent that for the first time a trip to Australia could be regarded as a holiday for some. In 1861 the ship

◄◄ The scene at Balaklava with troop and supply ships crowding into Cossack Bay during the Crimean War. (LoC)

◄ On his way to the Crimea, an army officer reads a letter in his cabin.

took the first English cricket team to tour Australia – although they couldn't practise on board – and a couple of years later Dr W.G. Grace took part in the second tour. In 1871 the author Anthony Trollope used his time on board, during a trip a visit to his son in Australia, to write the story *Lady Anna*.

On the trips back to the UK the *Great Britain* carried some returning passengers, although usually less than on the outward trip, and a variety of cargoes including wool and also gold – up to 7 tons of gold on one trip alone. She made her final voyage to Australia in 1876 and it is estimated that by then she had carried around 15,000 emigrants Down Under and that 250,000 or more modern Australians can trace their forebears back to the ship.

A TROOPSHIP

On two occasions the *Great Britain* was diverted from her Australian sojourns and chartered by the British Government as a troopship. In 1854 she spent ten months ferrying personnel and supplies between Malta and the Crimea, and in 1857 she also took troops to Bombay during the Sepoy Wars. If you view the forward hold of the restored ship you will see that the soldiers' horses were also carried on board. The animals were lowered into the hold in a harness and remained in the harness for most of the trip to prevent them from falling.

This vessel has a history of more than ordinary interest. It was offered for sale by Messers Kellock & company at their sale room … For a sailing ship her beautiful lines particularly adapt her and with her machinery taken out she is calculated to carry 4,000 tons deadweight.

Liverpool Mercury, 1881 report on the unsuccessful auction held at Birkenhead

In 1881 the *Great Britain* was put up for auction yet again, and a report in the *Liverpool Mercury* summed up her potential role and condition: 'although this steamer has been built many years her iron is so good and strength of construction so great that with a certain outlay she could be made a most desirable merchant ship.'

Despite this the bidding only reached £6,000 and the ship was withdrawn from the sale. Later that year it became the property of Antony Gibbs & Sons when they absorbed the previous owners, Gibbs, Bright & Co., and the following year they transferred ownership to Vicary Gibbs. The main engines were taken out and holes were cut in the engine room bulkheads to connect with the cargo

The Great Britain's third career was as a sailing ship.

holds; the funnels were dismantled, all passenger accommodation was removed, including the wooden superstructure, and new hatches were fitted for the loading of cargo. The rig remained much the same apart from the position of the main mast, which was moved forward. At this time the hull was sheathed in pine. The exact reason for this expensive operation has never been determined but presumably it was to reinforce the iron hull – perhaps to protect it from smaller fender vessels pulling up alongside and bumping against the outward bulge of the hull.

In November 1882 the *Great Britain* was registered in Liverpool as a cargo ship with a gross tonnage of 2,640. On 2 December 1852 she set off on her first voyage as a windjammer with a cargo of 3,292 tons of coal destined for San Francisco. All was not well at first and, after putting in to Montevideo, 200 tons of coal were removed and the rest was redistributed within the hold to improve stability. Lying low in the water, the hull had a tendency to wallow. Nearly six months elapsed before her arrival in San Francisco – a disappointingly slow voyage for a ship that had previously circled the world on the Australia run in far less time. On the return journey she carried wheat, bound for Cork in Ireland, and arrived back in January 1884. A second run with coal to San Francisco followed in the spring of 1884 and it proved to be another long, arduous voyage, with the ship not back to Cork until July 1885. Each round trip was taking approximately a year to complete.

▲ *In 1936 the* Great Britain *was scuttled at Sparrow Cove in the Falklands and left to rot.* (CMcC)

On 6 February 1886 the *Great Britain* set off from Cardiff with another cargo of coal, this time destined for Panama. By April they were nearing Cape Horn, on the southern tip of South America, when the ship ran into hurricane-force gales. The crew reported to the captain that the coal was shifting but he refused to put into port on the Falkland Islands. It was only later,

when another prolonged gale ripped away the fore and main topgallant masts, that he agreed to head into Port William.

Twice the bottom grounded out and a survey revealed that although the hull was still good the ship needed deck and spar repairs to the tune of £5,000. The money was not forthcoming and on 19 July 1887 the Lloyd's Register contained the entry 'Vessel converted to a hulk'. Her sailing days over, the old ship was sold to the Corporation of the Falklands Islands Company for £2,000 to serve as a floating wool and coal storehouse. There she lay, swinging with the wind at anchor. There were suggestions that the ship could be salvaged and returned to England, and the Governor of the Falklands launched an appeal, but the costs were too high and the scheme was abandoned. In 1936 she was

The unrestored forward section of the ship gives an impression of how big the hold would have been when she was used to carry cargo.

➤ The ship had been fitted with wire rigging originally, but this proved unsatisfactory and was replaced by conventional hemp rope.

➤➤ One of the massive wooden masts from her days as a windjammer, displayed alongside the ship.

Did you know?

On a typical run to Australia the ship would carry around 540 passengers, 140 crew, a cow, nearly 300 sheep, pigs and goats, plus more than 1,000 chickens, ducks, geese and turkeys.

towed to Sparrow Cove and finally scuttled with holes smashed into the iron hull to prevent her floating away. In her long and distinguished career the *Great Britain* had served in a wide variety of roles from luxury passenger liner, emigrant clipper, troop ship, windjammer to a coal hulk. It now looked as if Sparrow Cove was to be her grave.

A DISTINGUISHED WAR RECORD

The *Great Britain* was not entirely forgotten. During the First World War her coal had been used to refuel the Royal Navy's South Atlantic fleet, which defeated Admiral Graf von Spee's ships in the Battle of the Falkland Islands. She was also visited at Sparrow Cove during the Second World War, this time by the crew of HMS *Exeter*, who scavenged her iron plates to repair damage their ship had sustained in the Battle of the River Plate in December 1939. During the battle the *Exeter* had famously helped to defeat the German pocket battleship named after the admiral, *Graf Spee*. Thanks to the *Great Britain*'s iron plates, HMS *Exeter* made it safely back to England to fight again.

◁ In 1939 the Great Britain *was visited at Sparrow Cove by the crew of HMS* Exeter *who took some of her iron plates to make essential repairs to their ship, which had been damaged in the Battle of the River Plate.*

> The *Great Britain* is in surprisingly sound overall condition … The hull is in a favourable position for floating off and removal … The *Great Britain* is capable of salvage, the work should be within the compass of two or three months at Stanley for a salvage tug and crew, and the ship is very well worth the effort.
>
> Ewan Corlett, *Survey Report SS Great Britain Project*, 1968

Abandoned in Sparrow Cove, the *Great Britain*'s wooden masts and main spar – relics from her days as a windjammer – still rose tall and proud, but even a ship as strong as the *Great Britain* could not lie abandoned forever without deteriorating. For the Falklanders she had become an old friend. They would sometimes row out to the old ship to explore or have picnics, sometimes to collect fresh mussels from her hull. Few could have imagined that she would ever move from this spot, but by the 1960s concerns about her future and the need to salvage the ship began to emerge on both sides of the Atlantic. The director of the San Francisco Maritime Museum, Karl Kortum, visited the Falklands in 1967 to look over the *Great Britain* with a view of taking her to San Francisco or, preferably, returning her to the UK. Unknown to Kortum, in Britain the naval architect Ewan Corlett had a letter published in *The Times* in November that same year also calling for the recovery of the hulk, or at very least to have a full documented survey made of her. His pleas attracted support from a number of interested people and the SS Great Britain Project was formed in May 1968. At

◁ By the 1960s time was running out if the Great Britain *was going to be saved. (SWNA)*

➤ *The crack on the starboard side shows through the wooden cladding. (SWNA)*

➤➤ *The masts have been taken down as the ship is prepared for the salvage operation. The windlass can be seen in the foreground. (SWNA)*

this point Karl Kortum graciously conceded Britain's rightful claim to the grand old lady.

The immediate task for the SS Great Britain Project was to inspect the ship to ascertain the chances of moving her safely and in November 1968 Ewan Corlett headed a survey team, ably assisted by the Royal Navy and the crew of HMS *Endurance*. What they saw at Sparrow Cove was mostly encouraging. Yes, the hull had suffered a 30ft-wide crack on the starboard side, but the main part of the

> In position on the pontoon, ready to be raised. (SWNA)

hull was intact and resting on a bed of hard sand. Corlett's report concluded that the ship was in surprisingly sound condition and the hull was in a favourable position to be floated off. However he also realised that they had maybe five years at most before her condition deteriorated too far for her to be moved.

There were two options for salvaging the *Great Britain*. The first was to make

the hull watertight and tow her home – a highly risky plan given the ship's condition. The alternative was to use a new method being developed by the Anglo-German engineering company Risdon Beazley Ulrich Harms, which involved floating the vessel over a sunken pontoon and then raising it to the surface to carry the ship. A further survey by a towing company confirmed that the ship might not survive a direct tow and the pontoon method was decided on.

◀ Under tow on her final journey across the Atlantic Ocean. (SWNA)

▼ This side view of the hull riding on the Ulrich Harms pontoon conveys something of the scale of the salvage operation. (CMcC)

Even so, the chances of success were only put at 80 per cent. Finance for the scheme came mainly from the businessman Jack Hayward and in January 1970 the pontoon *Mulus III* left Liverpool in tow behind the tug *Varius II*.

At Sparrow Cove the *Great Britain* was prepared for her journey home. The heavy wooden masts together with the enormous 105ft-long iron spar were taken down, and the scuttling holes and the crack in the side of the hull were patched. Corlett had anticipated that the crack would close up once the hull had been lifted. After delays caused by the typically unpredictable Falklands weather, the *Great Britain* was finally floated on to the pontoon on 11 April 1970. The following day work began on pumping out the mud and silt and, as predicted, the hull straightened and the crack began to close. Two days later the water in the pontoon was pumped out and it lifted the ship clear out of the water. After a brief stay in Stanley to prepare her for the voyage, the *Great Britain* set off on her final transatlantic crossing on 24 April 1970. She stopped briefly in Montevideo on the way and arrived in Avonmouth Docks on 24 June, where she was un-docked from the pontoon a few days later.

Did you know?
Problems with the *Great Britain*'s compass, caused by the iron hull, may have been responsible for the ship running aground at Dundrum Bay.

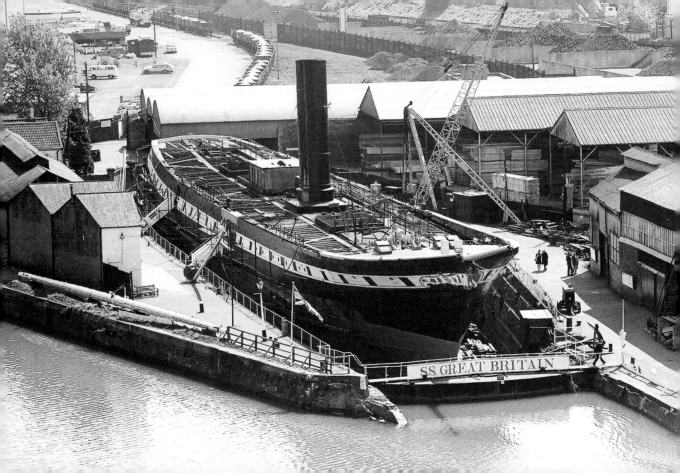

For tens of thousands of Bristolians it was an emotional moment when the great ship, floating on her own without assistance, was towed up the River Avon and under Brunel's now-completed Clifton Suspension Bridge. On the high tide of 5 July the *Great Britain* passed through the Cumberland Basin – this time without incident – and entered the Floating Harbour, where she was moored for two weeks while final preparations to receive her were made at the Great Western Dry Dock. Getting her back into the dock was going to be tricky as the keel had been extended with the additional wooden keels added in the 1852 refit. The hull was also sitting about 18in lower at the stern. Water was pumped out to get the ship level and she was carefully manoeuvred backwards into the dock with only inches to spare. It was 19 July 1970 – exactly 127 years to the day since her launch in 1843. Prince Albert had been present on that occasion and for this final stage of her long journey his modern counterpart, HRH Prince Philip, was on board to observe the proceedings.

The *Great Britain* had come home and now the hard work of preserving and restoring the ship could begin. But even in this moment of triumph a question mark hung over her future. Would she be allowed to stay in Bristol?

◁ *Back in her dry dock, the replica funnel is in place but the weather deck has yet to be fitted. Compare this scene with the image on p.41 to see how the new developments have filled this part of the docks. (JC)*

RESTORATION

SS *Great Britain* got our unanimous vote for being outstanding at every level. It combines a truly ground-breaking piece of conservation, remarkable engineering and fascinating social history plus a visually stunning ship above and below the water line.

Professor Robert Winston, chairman of the judging panel for the Gulbenkian Prize for Museums and Galleries, 2006

Restoring, or in this case reconstructing, a 322ft-long hulk that had been lying abandoned since 1936 was always going to be a mammoth task. At first sight the newly repatriated *Great Britain* looked a mess. Her wooden masts had been lopped off, the deck and the other woodwork was rotten, and the hull was covered in the wooden cladding applied when she became a windjammer. The immediate priority was to strip her down, clean her up and make her watertight. The incidental task, to make the ship presentable and turn her into an attraction that visitors would pay to see, wasn't so difficult. Even when stripped bare this was a fascinating vessel and like many people I remember clambering about the ship in the early 1970s before the weather deck was fitted.

First of all, they had to removes tons of mud from the interior; a far more delicate operation than you might imagine as it contained a number of hidden artefacts, including an original anchor. Removing the flaking rust and the accumulated scale and shellfish from the ironwork was a more brutal affair, involving high-pressure hoses, after which it was dried with flame jets and

> *A cornucopia of decorative detailing at the stern.*

then painted. Most of the woodwork had to be replaced and a new weather deck was urgently needed to protect the interior of the hull. With the appearance of a replica funnel and the six masts she started to look like a ship again.

At first the plan was to restore the *Great Britain* to her 1843 as-launched condition,

▶ *Prince Philip had been on board when the* Great Britain *entered the dry dock and he took a keen interest in her restoration. (SWNA)*

▶▶ *No weather deck yet, but a very smart circular skylight was in place to give visitors an idea of how the ship would appear eventually.*

but this philosophy was changed when it became obvious that the salvaged ship told a far bigger story of her career at sea rather than just a single point in history. In practical terms, this meant that below decks the emphasis was put on recreating enough of the interior to give visitors an impression of life on board. An early decision was made not to duplicate work by restoring both aft and forward promenade and dining areas. This also left space at the front half of the ship to serve as staff areas, meeting rooms, access corridors and so on, mostly hidden from view of the visitors. The area beneath the funnel, for example, houses the lift for disabled visitors. Tucked away elsewhere there are toilets and, in response to modern safety requirements, additional exit points have been created. Right at the front of the ship the full height of the interior was left as an open space and today this gives an inside view of the ship's construction. It also preserves a sense of how the hull appeared after her return to Bristol in 1970 as it shows the wafer thin condition of some of the iron plating in the lower hull where the light shines through like a constellation of distant stars.

As the work continued on the ship there were serious concerns about whether the Great Western Dry Dock would actually become her permanent home. The Corporation of Bristol was undecided about the future of the city docks, which were still commercially active then, and consequently the dry dock was on a short lease at first. Thankfully, alternative plans to build a road crossing on the site were eventually abandoned and the ship could remain where it was. Since then the *Great*

Britain has been at the forefront of the regeneration of the dock area and she has become one of the city's most recognisable icons.

By the early 1990s the restoration programme was starting to run out of steam, well funds actually, but by happy coincidence the Heritage Lottery Fund was just gearing into action. The ship's trustees took the shrewd decision to become a registered museum and Lottery backing enabled a new phase of restoration to

◄ *The restored first-class promenade saloon.*

Did you know?
Injuries among the crew were common on board ships, especially when dealing with the sails and rigging. On one transatlantic voyage the ship's surgeon had to amputate a seaman's arm.

begin. When the city council allowed the Great Western Dockyard to be bought back by the charitable trust, the *Great Britain*'s future in Bristol was finally assured.

This second phase of restoration is most notable for the glass roof which was installed between the hull and dock walls to establish a controlled environment to protect the vulnerable lower hull from the onslaught of rust – see *The Wrong Sort of Rust*. Elsewhere great emphasis has been put on contextualising or interpretation of

the various restored areas, using realistic figures to evoke the story of life on board. So in one cabin you might encounter a gentleman being shaved by his servant and in the next there is a mother with her young children. Restoring a historic vessel as important as the *Great Britain* requires a delicate balance in meeting the ship's needs and those of the visitor without straying into the realms of pastiche. For practical reasons she couldn't have been kept as a rusty hulk, it simply wouldn't have survived, and although I am very glad I got to see the old girl before she was restored I have to say she looks pretty good after the makeover.

One of the most striking achievements has been in the engine room. With the support of the Millennium Commission and Rolls-Royce plc, a full-scale model of

◄◄ One of the many cabins which hint of life at sea in the ship's transatlantic heyday.

◄ Looking up through the iron beams and one of the skylights.

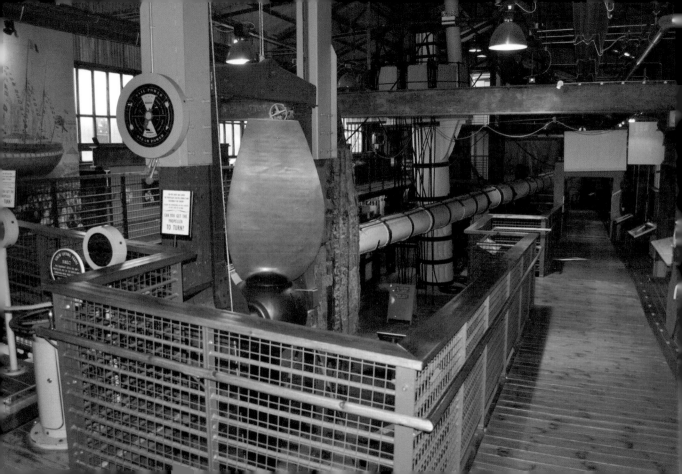

the steam engine was constructed using modern materials so as not to overload the old ship. Unveiled in 2006, it now fills the three-deck-high space with its movement and its reassuring throbbing sound. Since installation the new engine has revolved 2.7 million times, in effect travelling even further than the original, and in 2011 it was stopped for a well-deserved overhaul.

Located beside the *Great Britain*, one of the old dock buildings has been converted into a museum to display a wealth of material covering all periods of the ship's story, from her construction and launch to her return to Bristol. Dominating this area is the huge iron spar which was brought back with the ship from the Falklands and a replica of the 1857 tow-bladed screw which could be raised or lowered to reduce resistance when the ship was under sail. This display also affords the chance to learn about some of the individual experiences of those who sailed or served on her. There are many artefacts from the *Great Britain*, but also a few surviving items from Brunel's other ships, the *Great Western* and even the *Great Eastern*. Both of these vessels were broken up after their useful lives came to an end. We are very fortunate that this fate did not befall the *Great Britain*, and deservedly its restoration and presentation has won the project a number of prestigious heritage and conservation awards in recent years.

The iron which had been the source of much wonder in her early years, and which had given her the strength to weather many an Atlantic storm, was finally proving her downfall. The ship's iron hull had been subjected to continuous aggressive chloride attack from seawater.

Robert Turner, *Icon News*, 2005

Rust is nasty stuff, and unfortunately the wrought-iron hull of the *Great Britain* had plenty of it. And it was the wrong sort of rust.

The initial measures taken to clean and preserve the hull had been fine, up to a point. It had been cleaned with pressure washers, dried out as best as possible, patched up and painted. For an old car this might have been enough, but the rust eating away at the *Great Britain* was far more insidious by nature. After so many years of being pickled in sea water, the lower part of the hull was impregnated with salts which had bonded with the metal and continue to attract water to continue the corrosion process. To make matters worse the ship was located in the worst possible location. The Great Western Dry Dock had enormous historic significance for the ship, but it was only dry in name and not in practice. It would be almost impossible to stem the constant influx of moisture that naturally seeped through the fabric of its walls. Adding to the problem, the ship was completely exposed to the elements. Bristol has its fair share of rainy weather and the level of humidity, the amount of

➤ *An unexpected view of the ship's prow.*

➤ *High-pressure water jets were the most effective and least harmful means of cleaning the iron hull. (SWNA)*

Did you know?

The atmosphere in the dry dock beneath the *Great Britain*'s glass sea is said to be as dry as the Arizona Desert.

invisible moisture that the air can hold, is quite high.

By 1998 new research conducted by Cardiff University indicated that unless the corrosion was halted it would continue to eat away at the metal and could destroy the ship in as little as twenty years. If this scenario was left to run its course the ironwork would have to be replaced bit by bit until all that remained was a replica of the *Great Britain*. This has already happened with some preserved ships, such as HMS *Victory* in Portsmouth, which, after years of restoration and progressive replacement of its timber, is only about 20 per cent original. Hearts of oak might survive such drastic surgery unnoticed, but with the *Great Britain* the original iron plates and framework are its very essence. If the ship couldn't be moved to

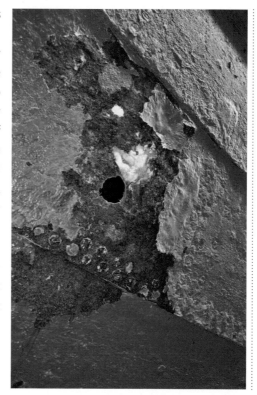

One of many holes in the flaking iron plating on the starboard side which remind visitors of the ship's fragility.

These ducts blow warm, dry air over the lower hull.

Deep Thought II is actually a pair of dehumidifiers that keep the atmosphere as dry as the Arizona Desert.

a drier environment – physically impossible as the hull is too fragile, and aesthetically undesirable given the dry dock's historic significance – then the existing environment would have to be modified. To accomplish this, a vast dehumidification chamber would

➤ *Close-up of an air duct nozzle.*

Did you know?

The *Great Britain* is one of Bristol's star tourist attractions, with around 170,000 visitors every year. That's almost 500 times the number of passengers she was designed to accommodate.

be constructed around the ship and the lower hull would be kept in a controlled environment with only 20 per cent humidity. This is roughly the equivalent of the Arizona Desert and, in comparison, Bristol's natural humidity is nearer 80 per cent.

Over a three-year period the hull was meticulously cleaned and the fibreglass patches covering hundreds of holes were replaced with less obtrusive resin repairs. A glass roof was installed to create a watertight and airtight seal between the dry dock and the hull and down below the dehumidifier, known as Deep Thought II, works tirelessly recycling the air and passing it through a water-absorbing chemical filter before blowing dry air out over the length of the hull via a series of nozzles.

Any concerns that this would adversely affect the character of the ship and its setting were instantly dispelled once the dry dock reopened to the public. In a stroke of genius, the glass ceiling has been covered in a thin layer of water, only an inch or two deep, which creates the illusion that the ship is floating in the dock. Even better, the

◄◄ *A fantastic perspective on Brunel's iron maiden.*

◄ *Sunlight dapples on the huge caisson which keeps the harbour's water at bay. This would be floated out of the way to allow vessels in and out of the dry dock.*

glass roof has actually enhanced the visitor experience. Standing on the dockside and looking down through the ripples of water there is a wonderful sense of peering into a massive surreal aquarium as you see figures walking around the hull. Descending into the chamber is equally magical. There is the sudden change of atmosphere as you enter the warm cocoon of desert-like air. Your senses are hit on two levels. Firstly by the enormity of the ship that hangs overhead fitting the dock like a well-worn glove, and secondly by the childlike experience of moving about a magic underwater world filled with dappled sunlight.

Being able to walk around the underside of the *Great Britain* is an almost unique experience when it comes to preserved historical vessels. It is a chance to see the incredible iron construction close up, including the untreated holes and the crude repairs made to the crack on the starboard side. At the rear of the ship a replica of the original six-bladed propeller looks magnificent in a coat of bright orange paint. Initially this had been displayed with the wooden rudder which had been on the ship when it returned to Bristol, but this rudder has now been moved to the museum building and a replica of Brunel's original is in its place. At the front of the ship you have a unique view looking up at the sharp prow, the cutting edge of this great ship, and one of the massive iron anchors is displayed nearby. It is said that when the anchor was dropped the noise of the chains was like thunder.

While underwater, it is worth taking a look at the dry dock itself. This was no mean feat of engineering in itself when

◀ *Ripples on the water and through time.*

Did you know?
If action hadn't been taken to protect it, the ship's hull could have been eaten away by rust in another twenty years.

Did you know?

When the *Great Britain* returned to its dry dock in Bristol on 19 July 1970, it was exactly 127 years to the day after she had been launched from there, and 133 years since the launch of the *Great Western* less than a mile away.

excavated in 1839. The walls of the dry dock feature wide ledges called altars which were used to rest the wooden staves that supported the ship during construction. The smaller steps in the walls provided access for the workmen. The dock has been widened and modified over the years when Bristol remained an active harbour for boat-building and repairs, and also for the timber and sand trade, until the late 1970s. The dock also suffered bomb damage during the Second World War. At its head is the caisson, a sturdy metal box that keeps out the harbour's water. This is floated upwards to fill the dry dock with water and allow the ships to pass in and out.

More recently the dockside surrounding the ship has been dressed with coils of rope, supplies in crates and the piled up luggage of transatlantic passengers waiting to board. It is a welcome distraction from the encroaching new buildings that surround the site, and an evocative reminder of an age when steam-powered ocean liners ruled the Atlantic.

1806 Birth of Isambard Kingdom Brunel.

1837 Brunel's first great ship, the wooden-hulled *Great Western*, launched in Bristol.

1839 Excavation of the Great Western Dry Dock and construction of the SS *Great Britain* commences.

1840 The propeller-driven *Archimedes* visits Bristol and Brunel abandons paddles for the new ship in favour of a screw propeller.

1841 Great Western Railway opened all the way from London to Bristol.

1843 19 July: *Great Britain* is launched.

1845 Maiden voyage to New York.

1846 Ship runs aground at Dundrum Bay on the Irish coast.

1849 The ship is sold to Gibbs, Bright & Co.

1851 Refitted to carry passengers to Australia.

1852 First of thirty-two voyages to Australia.

1854 Used as a troop transport during the Crimean War.

1857 Carries troops to India.

1859 Launch of the *Great Eastern* and death of I.K. Brunel.

1876 *Great Britain*'s last trip to Australia.

1882 Converted to a sailing ship and carries coal to San Francisco.

1886 The ship is damaged off Cape Horn and beached in Sparrow Bay in the Falklands. Sold as a hulk for coal and wool storage.

1914 First World War: British warships refuel from the ship prior to the Battle of the Falklands.

1939 Second World War: Iron plates taken from the ship to repair HMS *Exeter* after the Battle of the Plate.

1969 Ewan Corlett's salvage team surveys the ship.

1970 The *Great Britain* returns to Bristol.

Overall length	322ft (98m)
Width/beam	50ft 6in (15.39m)
Height keel to weather deck	32ft 6in (9.91m)
Draught	16ft (4.9m)
Displacement	3,675 tons load draught
Iron weight	1,040 tons
1845 propeller	16ft diameter (4.9m)
Masts	Six as built, five schooner-rigged and one square-rigged
	After 1853, three square-rigged
Speed	10–12 knots (12–13mph or 19–20km/h)
Engine	1,000hp, max. 20rpm
Load capacity	360 passengers as built, later increased to 730
	1,200 tons of cargo
Fuel capacity	1,200 tons of coal
Crew	130 officers and crew as built

Bilge	The lowest part of the hull where the sides meet the keel.
Bowsprit	Mast extending from the bow.
Caisson	The moving gate or door into a canal or dry dock.
Deadweight	A ship's carrying capacity with crew and supplies.
Forecastle	Deck area near the bow, also called the fo'c'sle.
Hold	Storage area in the lowest level of the hull.
Keel	The central spine of the hull running its full length.
Spar	Horizontal pole from which the sails are set.
SS	Stands for steamship, not screw-ship.
Topgallant	The upper portion of a mast.
Transom	Flat decorated part of the ship's stern.
Windlass	Mechanism to haul ropes or the anchor.
Yards	Cross pieces from which the square sails are hung.

◄ *There is very little external decoration on the ship apart from on the prow and here at the stern.*

APPENDIX 4 – FURTHER READING

Brunel – The Man Who Built the World by Steven Brindle, Weidenfeld & Nicolson.

Brunel's Kingdom – In the Footsteps of Britain's Greatest Engineer by John Christopher, The History Press.

The Iron Ship – The Story of Brunel's SS Great Britain by Ewan Corlett, Conway Maritime Press.

The Voyages of the Great Britain – Life at Sea in the World's First Liner by Nicholas Fogg, Chatham Publishing.

The Ocean Railway – Brunel, Samuel Cunard and the Revolutionary World of the Great Atlantic Steamships by Stephen Fox, Harper Perennial.

Brunel – In Love with the Impossible by Andrew & Melanie Kelly (eds), Brunel 200.

Isambard Kingdom Brunel – Recent Works by Kentley, Hudson & Peto (eds), Design Council.

Isambard Kingdom Brunel by L.T.C. Rolt, Penguin Books.

➤ *End view: the replica screw and rudder.*

Other titles available in this series

THE HMS VICTORY STORY

■ ISBN 978 07524 5605 8

THE QE2 STORY

■ ISBN 978 07524 5094 0

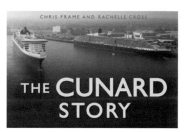

THE CUNARD STORY

■ ISBN 978 07524 5914 1

THE QM2 STORY

■ ISBN 978 07524 5092 6

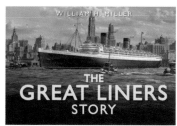

THE GREAT LINERS STORY

■ ISBN 978 07524 6452 7

THE MARY ROSE STORY

■ ISBN 978 07524 6404 6